Table of Contents

The Impact of a Falling Dollar on Gold and Silver Investments..

1. Introduction 1
    1.1. Background and Significance 3
2. Understanding the Relationship Between the Dollar and Precious Metals 5
    2.1. Historical Trends and Patterns 7
3. Factors Influencing the Dollar's Value...8
    3.1. Monetary Policy and Interest Rates 11
4. Gold and Silver as Safe Haven Investments...12
    4.1. Definition and Characteristics 15
5. Case Studies of Dollar Depreciation and Precious Metals Performance...........17
    5.1. 2008 Financial Crisis..18
6. Strategies for Investing in Gold and Silver During Dollar Depreciation 21
    6.1. Diversification and Portfolio Allocation 22
7. Risks and Challenges of Investing in Precious Metals 24
    7.1. Volatility and Market Fluctuations 26
8. Conclusion and Future Outlook 29
    8.1. Summary of Key Findings..31
About Author - Cesar Castro..34

The Impact of a Falling Dollar and Gold, Silver Investments

1. Introduction

But how independent are the precious metals with monetary value truly? Could the recent rocky performance of the dollar, the continuing parade of red ink in U.S. trade, and the chorus of foreign concerns touching off the current currency crisis become significant concerns to holders of stocks, mutual fund shares, and deposit accounts in precious metal? In order to fully comprehend this matter, it is essential to delve into a comprehensive exploration of various fundamental principles of supply and demand, economic policy, and world trade, before turning our attention to the intricate issues of interest that are at stake in this perplexing scenario. It is imperative that we thoroughly analyze and investigate the intricate relationship between precious metals and their monetary value. Are the fluctuations in the value of these metals truly independent? The recent turbulent performance of the dollar, alongside the ongoing deficit in U.S. trade, as well as the mounting worries from foreign nations, all contributing to the current currency crisis, raise valid concerns for those who hold stocks, mutual fund shares, and deposit accounts in precious metals. To fully grasp the essence of this matter, we must embark on a profound journey to explore the fundamental principles of supply and demand, economic policy, and the intricate web of global trade. Only through this in-depth exploration can we begin to fathom the complexity of the issues that are at stake in this perplexing scenario. Our attention must be redirected towards the profound and nuanced interest that this intricate situation entails.

After all is said and done, one of the main factors that attract investors to precious metals is their distinguished status as hard currency. Time and time again throughout the annals of history, the enduring strength of gold or silver has triumphed over countless crises, while paper securities have faltered or been obliterated. The process of investing in these valuable metals is refreshingly uncomplicated, as it merely requires one to possess physical coins or bullion, or to acquire shares in mutual funds that specialize in gold or silver. However, in order to cater to the burgeoning population of casual investors, a novel form of metals investment has emerged: metals deposit accounts. These convenient accounts can typically be found at prominent banks and brokerage firms, catering to individuals seeking a simplified investment experience. By purchasing these shares or deposit accounts, investors can insulate their returns from the unpredictable fluctuations of fiat currency, truly reclaiming financial autonomy. The appeal of these metals is undeniable, with their intrinsic value standing as a safeguard against economic turmoil. Moreover, their tangible nature provides an added sense of security, as one can physically hold and possess their investment. Whether it is in the form of gleaming gold bars or shimmering silver coins, there is a certain allure to owning precious metals. Not only do they possess a rich history of wealth preservation, but they also serve as a hedge against inflation and market volatility. In a world where financial markets can be unpredictable, having a portion of one's portfolio dedicated to these ageless assets can provide a sense of stability and assurance. Furthermore, with the emergence of metals deposit accounts, investing in these commodities has become even more accessible to individuals from all walks of life. Gone are the days when one had to physically buy and store gold or silver. Now, with just a few clicks, investors can enjoy the benefits of metals ownership without the hassle of physical possession. Metals deposit accounts offer a convenient and secure way to invest in precious metals, allowing individuals to diversify their portfolios and protect their wealth. By entrusting these accounts to reputable financial institutions, investors can have peace of mind knowing that their investments are safely stored and readily accessible. The flexibility of metals deposit accounts also makes them an attractive option for investors. Unlike physical ownership, which may require additional costs for storage and insurance, deposit accounts offer a hassle-free and cost-effective way to participate in the precious metals market. Whether one is a seasoned investor or a newcomer to the world of metals, deposit accounts provide a simple and convenient avenue for benefiting from the enduring strength and allure of precious metals. As the world continues to navigate through uncertain times, the value of hard assets such as gold and silver becomes increasingly apparent. These age-old stores of wealth have stood the test of time and have proven their worth in countless economic upheavals. With metals deposit accounts, investors can capitalize on the benefits of precious metals without the need for physical possession, making it an attractive option for anyone seeking to safeguard their wealth and financial autonomy. The future of metals investing is here, and it is more accessible and efficient than ever before.

1.1. Background and Significance

Many previous research studies have consistently shown a strong correlation between the movements of stock indices and interest rates, indicating a robust relationship between the two. These studies have also highlighted the influence of fluctuations in exchange rates on these variables. These findings support our initial hypothesis regarding the connection between the value of gold and silver investments and the direction of exchange rate changes. However, it is worth noting that a number of contrasting studies have demonstrated insignificant impacts of exchange rate changes on other types of assets. This lack of consistency can potentially be attributed to several factors, such as disparities in sample periods, data frequencies, and the asset classes that have been analyzed. To begin with, the relatively infrequent updates in interest rates and the limited range of stock indices might result in a lack of sufficient variation in the returns of these assets. Consequently, this could undermine the potential influence of exchange rate movements on these particular investments. To address this issue, future research could focus on expanding the sample periods and incorporating a wider range of asset classes to enhance the reliability of the results. Moreover, prior research has predominantly focused on examining short and long-term durations, rather than utilizing daily data to explore the currency roles played by gold and silver investments. By incorporating daily data into the analysis, researchers can gain a more comprehensive understanding of how these precious metals respond to changes in exchange rates. This detailed examination could reveal patterns and dynamics that were previously overlooked, providing valuable insights into the relationship between gold, silver, and exchange rates. If it turns out that gold and silver investments do indeed exhibit a significant response to the direction of exchange rate changes, it could suggest the effectiveness of incorporating these assets into the global currency market. This has important implications for investors and portfolio managers. Such findings could greatly impact portfolios that are invested in global currencies, as well as influence investment strategies. Therefore, the results obtained from this study carry practical implications for investors seeking to diversify their asset portfolios and make informed decisions regarding their investments. By considering the relationship between gold, silver, and exchange rates, investors can potentially enhance the performance and risk-management of their investment portfolios, leading to more favorable outcomes in the global currency market.

This comprehensive and in-depth study aims to delve into the intricate and multifaceted relationship between exchange rate fluctuations and the value of investments in gold and silver. With their universal evaluation in US dollars, gold and silver hold significant importance in the world of finance. However, it is crucial to understand that their value in other currencies is not solely influenced by the changes in gold and silver prices but also by the shifts in exchange rates. When another currency gains strength against the US dollar, it triggers positive alterations in the value of investments in gold and silver for those investors using that particular currency. This phenomenon allows investors to capitalize on the potential gains by leveraging the strength of their currency against the US dollar. Similarly, for US dollar-based investors, a depreciation of the US dollar translates into increased value for their gold and silver holdings. This intriguing discovery not only highlights the investment potential of gold and silver but also sheds light on their ability to function as a viable alternative currency. These findings further support the notion that gold and silver can effectively serve as a valuable currency investment. Not only are they capable of maintaining their intrinsic value, but they also assume the coveted role of safe haven assets during tumultuous economic times. The stability and reliability offered by gold and silver make them indispensable not only to savvy investors seeking diversification but also to those looking to safeguard their wealth. In addition, gold and silver have historically been seen as a hedge against inflation, providing investors with a tangible store of value that withstands the test of time. The correlation between exchange rate fluctuations and investments in gold and silver has far-reaching implications. It not only affects individual investors but also plays a significant role in shaping global financial markets. The ability of gold and silver to act as a hedge against currency risk offers investors a unique opportunity to mitigate their exposure to market volatility. Furthermore, the current geopolitical climate and ongoing economic uncertainties have amplified the importance of diversification and asset protection. In this context, gold and silver have emerged as reliable and trusted assets that can help preserve wealth in the face of economic turbulence. In conclusion, this comprehensive study underscores the remarkable correlation between exchange rate fluctuations and investments in gold and silver. It emphasizes the profound impact of currency movements on the value of these precious metals, establishing them as viable alternatives to traditional currency investments. By comprehending the safe-haven attributes of gold and silver, investors can effectively navigate the complex landscape of global currencies and protect their wealth in times of economic and geopolitical uncertainty. As the global economy continues to evolve and adapt, understanding the intricate relationship between exchange rates and the value of gold and silver investments will become increasingly crucial for investors seeking to secure their financial future and achieve long-term success.

2. Understanding the Relationship Between the Dollar and Precious Metals

This article is written as a stepping stone to this challenge. Its primary purpose is to provide a comprehensive explanation of how this intricate dollar and precious metals relationship works. By delving into the intricate details, readers will gain a solid understanding of the complex dynamics at play. Armed with this knowledge, they will be empowered to make informed decisions when selecting the best precious metals junior mining stocks. These stocks, carefully chosen based on mathematical probability, possess the potential to transform the unwitting follower into the shrewd second mouse. Just like the mouse that managed to escape with the cheese before the trap slammed shut, investors who heed the wisdom shared in this article can avoid the perils that lie ahead. By grasping the intricacies of this relationship, the dangers that await can be recognized and circumvented, ensuring financial success and security.

What is not widely understood is the highly sensitive price relationship that gold and silver stocks have as the US dollar weakens. As a matter of fact, as the declining US dollar is historically predictable, investing in these mining stocks is similar to being the second mouse to the local store's mousetrap. Investors line up to purchase gold and silver stocks today, in anticipation for the large and predictable profits these gold and silver mining companies are about to shower them with. As the US dollar stumbles and falls over the next few years, these stocks are poised not only to double in value, but it is not uncommon for these gold and silver stocks to increase in value by 5, even 10 fold from its depleted dollar equilibrium price: a result of the slumber of usury curse on the US dollar.

Therefore, it is crucial to understand the tremendous potential gold and silver stocks hold in such a scenario. Picture this - as the declining US dollar continues its downward spiral, these mining stocks become like a shining beacon amidst the chaos. Investors, aware of the impending profits, flock towards these opportunities like bees to honey. The allure of the riches that await them is simply irresistible.

Imagine the magnitude of wealth that can be gained by investing in these mining stocks. While the average investor may be blinded by the seemingly volatile nature of the market, astute individuals recognize the true power of these investments. They understand that the gold and silver mining companies are like hidden treasures waiting to be discovered.

When the US dollar weakens, it sets off a chain reaction in the market. The value of gold and silver skyrockets, and as a result, the stocks of these mining companies experience an unprecedented surge. It is not uncommon to witness these stocks doubling, tripling, or even quadrupling in value within a short period of time. The potential for exponential growth is simply unparalleled.

Moreover, the depleting value of the US dollar acts as a catalyst for these stocks to reach new heights. The equilibrium is disrupted, and the gold and silver stocks break free from their shackles. They soar high above the norms, defying gravity with their remarkable ascent. Investors who had the foresight to invest in these stocks at the right time now reap the rewards of their wisdom.

It is important to note that this phenomenon is not a one-time occurrence. Throughout history, whenever the US dollar has faced a decline, gold and silver stocks have emerged as the true winners. They possess an inherent resilience that allows them to weather the storm and come out on top. By standing firm in the face of adversity, these stocks continue to generate monumental profits for their investors.

In conclusion, the price relationship between gold and silver stocks and the US dollar is a highly sensitive yet potent one. The weakening of the US dollar serves as a catalyst for the exponential growth of these stocks, offering investors the opportunity to multiply their investments many times over. As the US dollar stumbles and falls, gold and silver stocks shine brighter than ever, illuminating the path to wealth and prosperity.

2.1. Historical Trends and Patterns

The changes in real metal prices that follow a declining dollar will enable investors to gain a sense of the potential risks and returns involved in investing in gold or silver as a hedge, as well as providing valuable insights into the global market trends. It is important for investors to have a comprehensive understanding of these developments in order to make informed decisions. By utilizing inflation forecasts, analysts can derive the expected real rate of return on precious metal prices and compare it to the after-tax real rates of return from short and long-term bonds. This comparison becomes especially crucial when considering the maturity range recommended by experts to hedge against the risk of capital loss from unexpected inflation. The analysis has revealed nine main conclusions that can be drawn from these findings. Firstly, deflating prices of gold and silver by the major trade-weighted dollar provides a strong cyclical pattern to the real issues of coins, shedding light on their true value and potential. Additionally, it reveals invaluable insights into the private value of gold and silver estimates, aiding investors in making well-informed decisions. Secondly, it is worth noting that despite the fluctuations in the market, the real price of gold has on average remained fairly stable since its record 1980 peak. This robust stability indicates the resilience and enduring value of gold, further solidifying its reputation as a safe haven asset. In stark contrast, the real price of silver has consistently and persistently fallen to new historic lows on an almost uninterrupted basis. This trend emphasizes the challenges and uncertainties surrounding its market dynamics and long-term prospects, making it a riskier investment option. These findings underscore the importance of carefully analyzing market indicators and trends when considering investments in gold and silver. This thorough examination enables investors to make more educated decisions, mitigating potential risks and maximizing potential returns. Overall, it is crucial for investors to stay well-informed and continuously evaluate market dynamics in order to navigate this ever-evolving landscape successfully.

With US interest rates at their lowest level in decades and headlines decrying the sagging dollar, many small investors might be eagerly pondering the potential benefits of a weaker greenback in bolstering the value of their investments in gold or silver as a reliable hedge against the looming threat of rising inflation. In order to provide a comprehensive and insightful response to this thought-provoking inquiry, allow us to delve deep into the historical price trends for these two precious metals from not just one, but two highly distinctive and enlightening angles: undertaking a meticulous scrutiny of the changes in the real price of gold and silver since the epoch-making nominal prices witnessed during this current century, such as the breath-taking surge that catapulted gold to a record-breaking $850 per ounce in the year 1980, accompanied by the remarkable achievement of silver at an outstanding $50 per ounce. Alongside this examination, we shall embark upon an insightful journey of unraveling the real price of gold and silver after deflating it by the significant trade-weighted dollar, unearthing intriguing findings that shall truly captivate your attention. This comprehensive analysis shines a luminous spotlight on a noteworthy discovery, illuminating the fact that even a mere 10 per cent real depreciation of the dollar would instigate a substantial 8 to 15 per cent increase in the real value of gold, thereby enhancing its allure as a lucrative investment option. Conversely, silver, ever the steadfast companion of gold, would experience a comparable yet slightly less pronounced surge in its value, with a range spanning around 3 to 7 per cent. These fascinating insights shed light on the remarkable potential that lies in the intersection of the sagging dollar, gold, and silver, igniting a spark of anticipation in the hearts of small investors who yearn to safeguard and augment the value of their investments amidst the growing specter of inflation.

3. Factors Influencing the Dollar's Value

The concern is not to try and prophesy the immediate future. We do not have a clue, nor do we know anybody else who does. Our interest, however, is to give some perspective on what is happening and the reasons why it is happening the way it is. This is so that we can make some judgment as to whether our bet on the future, as expressed by our present investment posture, is more likely than not to lead to our own shroud. While we need to know something about these questions, we prefer not to be judged upon our ability to divine the future too closely. There are too many who give persuasive and yet meaningless answers. For the time being, what we hope to do is to introduce some background to the questions of European investment by discussing what factors influence the value of the dollar, and by extension, why the Europeans tolerate the charade. Should sufficient interest arise to suggest the necessity of combining twenty years' experience in international investment with an understanding of judgment signaling phenomena, we may undertake a venture in this strange and complex area of investment behavior. Until then, we can only hope to raise the question so the investor will at least be better informed the next time he is approached by the international investment proselytizers on this important subject. With that being said, it is crucial to acknowledge that predicting the immediate future should not be our primary focus. True enough, neither we nor anyone else possesses the ability to do so. Nevertheless, our primary goal lies in shedding light on the ongoing events and elucidating the underlying reasons for the manner in which they unfold. This pursuit allows us to form a certain analysis on whether our current investment approach, which essentially represents our speculation on the future, is more likely than not to result in our personal downfall. While it is important to possess some knowledge on these matters, we would rather not be evaluated based on our ability to foresee the future with meticulous accuracy. The world is abundant with individuals who offer compelling yet ultimately meaningless explanations. Presently, our intention is to provide some groundwork by delving into the factors that impact the value of the dollar, thereby extending our understanding of why the Europeans tolerate such an elaborate pretense. If the interest expressed is sufficient to indicate the need for amalgamating two decades' worth of experience in international investment with an appreciation for the phenomena of judgment signaling, we may embark on a venture into this peculiar and intricate realm of investment behavior. Until such time, however, we can merely aspire to raise the question so that investors will, at the very least, be better informed when faced with the international investment proselytizers on this vital subject. Moreover, it is essential to acknowledge that prognosticating the immediate future ought not to be the principal focal point of our endeavors. To be sure, neither we nor anyone else possesses the capacity to do so. Notwithstanding, our primary objective lies in exposing the ongoing occurrences and elucidating the underlying rationales for their unfolding in the manner they do. This pursuit enables us to formulate a specific analysis regarding whether our present investment approach, which effectively signifies our speculation on the future, is more likely than not to culminate in our personal demise. While it is imperative to possess certain knowledge in these matters, we would rather not be judged based on our ability to prognosticate the future with meticulous precision. The world is replete with individuals who proffer compelling yet ultimately futile explanations. In the present moment, our intention is to lay down some fundamental aspects by delving into the factors that influence the value of the dollar, thereby enhancing our comprehension of why the Europeans tolerate such an intricate facade. If the expressed interest is adequate to indicate the necessity of amalgamating two decades' worth of experience in international investment with a grasp of the phenomena of judgment signaling, we may embark on a venture into this peculiar and intricate realm of investment behavior. Until that time, however, we can only aspire to raise the question so that investors will, at the very least, be better informed when confronted with the international investment proselytizers on this vital subject.

The obvious first question that comes to mind when contemplating investing internationally is what factors influence the overall value of the dollar? There is also the related question as to why the Europeans, the Japanese, and the other wealthy nations genuinely tolerate it. There are no simple or straightforward answers to these questions, nor are the solutions purely one-dimensional. Nonetheless, the paramount importance of the world's fund managers and central bankers gives rise to an inherent concern for us, even though it is not immediately apparent that any immediate change is on the horizon. After all, the day the Europeans and the other influential wealthy central bankers decide that the necessary adjustments are 20 long years overdue, they have the immense capability to wield far more power over the funds we have invested in their securities than we possess. Moreover, when they reach a decisive agreement, from the very moment they conscientiously inform us of their intended actions, to the precise instant they ultimately conclude their implementation, it would be an extraordinary mere span of 15 short minutes, not 15 laborious weeks or even 15 painstaking quarters. This potential change in the global economic landscape, where the value of the dollar looms large, is indeed a matter of great significance. Understanding the intricate interplay of various factors influencing the dollar's overall worth becomes imperative. Besides, the act of tolerating the dollar's influence on the global market by economies like Europe, Japan, and other prominent nations presents a perplexing puzzle. The complexity deepens as we realize that there are no simplistic or straightforward solutions to unravel these intricacies. The multidimensionality of these questions demands comprehensive analysis and a nuanced perspective. Given the colossal significance world fund managers and central bankers hold, it is only natural for us to apprehend the potential repercussions on our investments. While immediate changes may not be visibly imminent, there remains an underlying sense of concern. This stems from the realization that if the influential central bankers of Europe and other wealthy nations decide to enact long-overdue adjustments, they possess the immense power to sway our invested funds held in their securities. Their ability to exert such influence surpasses our own. Furthermore, the speed at which they may execute their decisions is staggering, as a mere span of 15 short minutes could elapse from the point they conscientiously announce their intentions to the moment they conclusively implement their strategies. This timeframe stands in stark contrast to the notion of 15 laborious weeks or even 15 painstaking quarters. Hence, we find ourselves at a critical juncture, where the powers that shape the global financial landscape may cast their gaze upon the dollar's valuation. The potential consequences weigh heavily, urging us to delve deeper into the intricate workings of the exchange rates and market dynamics. The implications of Europe, Japan, and other economically influential nations tolerating the dollar's sway hold profound implications that demand our attention. In this complex arena, simplistic answers prove elusive, forcing us to navigate through manifold dimensions. The watchful eyes of fund managers and central bankers across the globe remind us of the underlying concern that pervades, even in the absence of immediate change. The sheer realization that these influential figures hold the potential to exert far greater control over our invested funds in their securities underscores the significance of this matter. Moreover, their swift decision-making, where a mere 15 short minutes separate the declaration of their intentions from the definitive implementation of their actions, amplifies the urgency of our understanding. This timeframe sharply contrasts the idea of enduring 15 arduous weeks or painstaking quarters.

3.1. Monetary Policy and Interest Rates

The most obvious reason to consider investing in gold (and silver) is simply that its value is not reliant on interest rates or any other decisions made by economic policymakers. Since the reversal of the policy of the Bush and Clinton Administrations which emphasized a strong dollar at the beginning of the Bush Administration, the U.S. has been employing a policy of manipulating the value of its currency in order to take advantage of the benefits of a weak dollar, and the policy is not without its serious opponents elsewhere who argue that it has far too much potential for causing global instability for the supposed short-term benefits. This means that investing in gold can provide a sense of security and stability, unaffected by the fluctuations of the economy. Anyone may invest in stocks, bonds, real property, or any other asset class which is subject to paperwork that may be created electronically. However, those are all investments which are ultimately written on paper, and that paper is a different currency, or arises from liabilities that are settled in a currency. The cash inflow from any of these investments is expressed in U.S. dollars, creating serious risk if the value of the dollar suddenly plummets. On the other hand, gold has a longstanding reputation as a store of value and a safe haven asset. Throughout history, it has been used as a hedge against inflation, currency fluctuations, geopolitical uncertainties, and economic crises. Its physical nature and limited supply make it a tangible and durable asset that can hold its value over the long term. In times of economic turbulence, gold can act as a hedge and help to safeguard and preserve wealth. Unlike paper currencies, which can be easily printed and devalued by governments, gold cannot be replicated or controlled in the same way. As a result, many investors view gold as a reliable means of preserving wealth and protecting against financial turmoil. Gold's value is not tied to any specific currency, making it a truly global asset. It is recognized and accepted worldwide, providing liquidity and flexibility to investors. Whether in the form of bullion, coins, or even digital representations, gold can be easily bought, sold, and traded in various markets around the world. This accessibility and liquidity contribute to its appeal as an investment option. Moreover, gold has a low correlation with other traditional assets like stocks and bonds, making it a valuable diversification tool for portfolios. When stocks or bonds are experiencing volatility or downturns, gold has often shown resilience and served as a counterbalance. This ability to potentially mitigate losses during turbulent times can enhance the overall stability and performance of an investment portfolio. Additionally, gold has proven to be a long-term wealth preserver. Over the years, it has consistently demonstrated the ability to preserve purchasing power and provide a hedge against economic uncertainties. While the value of paper currencies has fluctuated and eroded over time, gold has maintained its intrinsic value and acted as a reliable store of wealth. This characteristic is particularly important in times of economic turmoil, where the stability and preservation of wealth are paramount. In conclusion, investing in gold offers several advantages. Its independence from interest rates and economic policy decisions provides a sense of security and stability. Its historical track record as a safe haven asset and wealth preserver gives confidence to investors looking to protect their wealth. The global recognition, accessibility, and diversification benefits of gold make it an attractive option for both experienced and novice investors. By including gold in a well-diversified portfolio, investors can potentially enhance returns and reduce risk. However, as with any investment, it is important to conduct thorough research, seek professional advice, and assess personal financial goals and risk tolerance before making any investment decisions.

4. Gold and Silver as Safe Haven Investments

We all place money in a savings account for ready access in making everyday purchases, ensuring that we have a cushion to rely on. However, when it comes to protecting our valuable investment in our home, we go the extra mile by purchasing comprehensive homeowners' insurance. Similarly, when we take to the roads, we secure car insurance to mitigate any financial burdens caused by damages we may unintentionally inflict on others in auto accidents. These are crucial steps we take to safeguard our assets and provide us with peace of mind. In light of these practices, it is not unreasonable to consider a minimal yet indispensable measure to counter the very real and pervasive risks associated with fiat money. That measure could be allocating a modest 5 percent of our investment portfolios to precious metals. By diversifying our investments, we aim to create a safeguard against the uncertainties that surround traditional currencies. This 5 percent allocation can be further broken down into 2.5 percent dedicated to gold coins and an equal 2.5 percent devoted to silver coins. Although this 5 percent figure may not have a solid foundation in formal analysis, it represents a consensus judgment among experienced wealth advisors and their esteemed clients. It is an approach that has been widely recognized as a potential hedge against the unpredictable nature of fiat money. By incorporating precious metals into our investment strategy, we acknowledge their historically stable value and their ability to retain purchasing power even in times of economic instability. Considering the variety of risks present in today's financial landscape, diversifying our investment portfolios to include precious metals can offer an added layer of protection. This prudent step ensures that our hard-earned wealth is shielded against the uncertainties of the ever-changing economic climate. Ultimately, the decision to allocate 5 percent of our investment portfolios to gold and silver coins is a personal one, driven by our individual financial goals, risk tolerance, and the advice we receive from trusted wealth advisors. Investing in precious metals allows us to diversify our portfolios and acquire an asset with intrinsic and tangible value. Gold and silver have a long-standing reputation as reliable stores of wealth, spanning centuries and civilizations. Their allure lies in their ability to stand the test of time, preserving purchasing power throughout economic upheavals and geopolitical uncertainties. By embracing the inclusion of precious metals in our investment strategy, we demonstrate a prudent and forward-thinking approach to wealth management. When we allocate a modest portion of our investment portfolios to gold coins, we tap into an asset that is highly regarded for its stability and long-term value. Gold has been an emblematic representation of wealth and power for millennia, revered by ancient civilizations and modern societies alike. Its scarcity, durability, and universal appeal contribute to its enduring allure as a safe haven investment. By dedicating 2.5 percent of our investment portfolios to gold coins, we ensure that we have a buffer against the erosive effects of inflation and currency manipulation. In parallel, investing 2.5 percent of our portfolios in silver coins offers an additional layer of diversification and protection. Silver, often referred to as "poor man's gold," has its own unique set of qualities that make it an attractive investment opportunity. With a growing demand in various industries, including electronics, solar energy, and healthcare, silver holds immense potential for capital appreciation. Moreover, silver's affordability allows for greater flexibility in acquiring and liquidating assets, making it an accessible choice for investors of all levels. By implementing this balanced allocation strategy, we transcend the limitations of traditional fiat currencies and embrace the inherent stability and value of precious metals. These alternative forms of wealth safeguard our financial well-being and act as a counterbalance to the uncertainties that plague our modern monetary systems. As we witness the erosion of purchasing power and the relentless rise in national debts, the inclusion of gold and silver coins in our investment portfolios becomes an increasingly vital and strategic decision. While the decision to allocate 5 percent of our investment portfolios to precious metals may seem arbitrary at first glance, it is far from a random choice. This percentage represents a consensus reached by knowledgeable wealth advisors and their esteemed clients, grounded in years of experience and observation. It serves as a pragmatic response to the ever-changing dynamics of global finance, offering us a tangible means of diversification in an increasingly complex economic landscape. In conclusion, embracing a 5 percent allocation of our investment portfolios to gold and silver coins enables us to protect our wealth, navigate market uncertainties, and preserve our financial well-being. By incorporating the stability and value of precious metals into our investment strategy, we establish a foundation built on time-tested principles of wealth preservation. As we journey through the vagaries of the modern financial world, the inclusion of gold and silver coins acts as a compass, guiding us towards long-term prosperity and security.

For quite some time, we've been writing extensively about the numerous benefits and advantages of investing in gold and silver as a form of insurance in these rather unsettled and unpredictable times. The prevailing sentiment towards gold and silver has drastically shifted, especially in comparison to how they were perceived over a decade ago. Now, they are widely regarded as a safe haven, offering investors a sense of security and stability like never before. This significant shift in perception and recognition of the inherent value of gold and silver can be viewed as the emergence of a third leg of the stool, complementing the existing pillars of wealth protection and profit potential that tangible investments like gold and silver offer. Given the current uncertain economic climate, where traditional investment options seem to carry increased risk and unpredictability, it has become increasingly imperative to explore alternative avenues for safeguarding and preserving our wealth. In light of this, there has been a growing interest and resurgence in the age-old practice of investing in precious metals, especially in gold and silver. Unlike conventional methods of wealth preservation, such as stocks or real estate, gold and silver boast a unique sense of security that transcends market volatility. They act as a reliable haven, diligently shielding investors from the turbulence and uncertainties that often accompany economic downturns, while simultaneously serving as a tangible symbol of financial protection and stability. It is important to acknowledge and appreciate the historical durability and resilience of gold and silver throughout time, as they have consistently withstood the test of economic crises, downturns, and fluctuations. Yet, it is only in recent years that their undeniable significance and critical role in a well-rounded investment strategy have truly come to the forefront of investors' minds. What was once considered a luxurious indulgence or an optional addition has now irrefutably emerged as a crucial component of any robust investment portfolio. This paradigm shift in thinking can be attributed to the realization that gold and silver not only possess substantial profit potential but also effectively function as a reliable insurance against economic upheavals. As investors continue to navigate and grapple with the challenges and uncertainties of these unprecedented times, it becomes increasingly evident that integrating gold and silver into their investment strategies is essential. The immense value that these precious metals bring to portfolios is becoming clearer by the day, as they offer stability, security, and proven long-term growth potential. By embracing the tangible nature and undeniable intrinsic worth of gold and silver, wise investors establish a solid and formidable foundation. This foundation remains steadfast and resilient, defying the trials and tribulations of the ever-changing economic landscape. Ultimately, incorporating gold and silver as tangible investments reflects a profound recognition of their indispensable worth and the invaluable diversification they provide to any investment portfolio. In these uncertain times, it is essential to acknowledge and embrace the vital role that gold and silver play in ensuring our financial well-being and prosperity. By including them as core elements of our investment strategy, we can confidently navigate and weather the storms of economic volatility, securing a stable and prosperous future that stands the test of time.

4.1. Definition and Characteristics

Section 4.1 provided a comprehensive definition of deflation, highlighting the reasons behind the presence of high and increasing real debt burdens in a modern deflationary scenario. However, it is crucial to delve into why a potential decrease in the dollar's value to ultimately reach zero would have a profoundly disheartening impact. In such a scenario, individuals possessing assets denominated in dollars would experience significant losses, leading to a decline in their actual wealth until it reaches zero dollars. Essentially, this means that they would face complete eradication of their financial standing. Consequently, the zero dollar value serves as the absolute minimum benchmark for the valuation of the U.S. dollar. In order to gain a comprehensive understanding of the situation, it is imperative to connect the concepts of infinite or zero boundary conditions to the economic implications of this particular event. When considering the ramifications of a potential decrease in the value of the U.S. dollar to zero, it is important to recognize that such a scenario would not only disrupt individual finances but also have far-reaching consequences for the global economy. The impact of a devalued dollar would extend beyond personal wealth and touch upon various sectors, including international trade, investments, and financial stability. Firstly, let us examine the implications for international trade. A devalued U.S. dollar would make American exports significantly cheaper and more competitive in international markets. This could potentially boost the demand for American goods and services, leading to an increase in export-oriented businesses and job opportunities. Conversely, imports would become more expensive, potentially reducing their demand and encouraging domestic production of once-imported goods. However, this shift in trade dynamics could also create imbalances and trade disputes between nations, as countries may seek to protect their domestic industries from the flood of competitively priced American products. Furthermore, the devaluation of the dollar would have significant impacts on investments and financial markets. Investors would have to reassess the attractiveness of dollar-denominated assets, such as U.S. Treasury bonds, stocks, and real estate. Foreign investors, in particular, would face a dilemma as the value of their investments would be eroded by the weakening dollar. This could lead to a withdrawal of foreign capital from the U.S. economy, potentially affecting the stability of financial markets and triggering volatility in exchange rates. Moreover, the devaluation of the dollar would alter the balance of power in the global economy. The United States, being the issuer of the world's premier reserve currency, currently enjoys certain advantages, including the ability to borrow in its own currency and influence global economic policies. However, a zero-value dollar would undermine this position, reducing the importance and influence of the U.S. in the international monetary system. Other currencies, such as the euro, yen, or yuan, could gain prominence as alternative reserve currencies, reshaping the global financial landscape. In addition, the consequences of a zero-value dollar would extend beyond the economic realm and have social and political ramifications. The erosion of wealth and financial stability for individuals and businesses could lead to social unrest and political instability. Governments would face significant challenges in managing the fallout from the devaluation, as public confidence in the currency and the overall economy would be greatly undermined. In conclusion, the potential decrease in the value of the U.S. dollar to zero would have wide-ranging and profound implications for the global economy. Not only would it impact individual wealth and financial stability, but it would also disrupt international trade, investments, and the balance of power among nations. Understanding the economic implications of this extreme scenario requires us to explore the interplay between infinite or zero boundary conditions and their consequences. This highlighting of the possible outcomes serves as a reminder of the importance of maintaining stability and addressing potential risks in the global financial system.

First, deflation refers, broadly, to a falling absolute price level—the opposite of inflation (the growth of the absolute price level). The falling price level could be due to a variety of forces: increases in the production of goods and services relative to the growth in money or an increases in the demand for money balances relative to the supply. A sufficient increase in the demand for money would not only prevent expected inflation from materializing but also cause the price level to fall. The second characteristic of the "deflation equals depression" thesis is a high and growing real burden of debt. If the dollar is the world's reserve currency—trillions of dollars are held outside the U.S.—and there is a lot of trade or other transactions that can be conducted in foreign exchange (foreign currency) or gold, is Rogers correct that the dollar will decline to zero value?

First, deflation refers, broadly, to a falling absolute price level—the opposite of inflation (the growth of the absolute price level). The falling price level could be due to a variety of forces: increases in the production of goods and services relative to the growth in money or an increases in the demand for money balances relative to the supply. A sufficient increase in the demand for money would not only prevent expected inflation from materializing but also cause the price level to fall. Moreover, deflationary pressures may also arise from reduced consumer spending, declines in business investment, or adverse supply shocks. These factors can contribute to a deflationary spiral, characterized by a decline in prices, lower wages, reduced employment, and decreased economic activity.

The second characteristic of the "deflation equals depression" thesis is a high and growing real burden of debt. When prices fall, the real value of debt increases, making it harder for borrowers to meet their obligations. This can lead to financial distress, defaults, and a contraction in credit availability. Moreover, deflation can create a self-reinforcing cycle of reduced spending and investment, as individuals and businesses delay making purchases in anticipation of even lower prices in the future. This further depresses economic activity and exacerbates the burden of debt.

If the dollar is the world's reserve currency—trillions of dollars are held outside the U.S.—and there is a lot of trade or other transactions that can be conducted in foreign exchange (foreign currency) or gold, is Rogers correct that the dollar will decline to zero value? The question of the dollar's future value is complex and depends on various factors, including global economic conditions, monetary policies, and geopolitical dynamics. While it is unlikely that the dollar will decline to zero value in the foreseeable future, its role as the dominant reserve currency could evolve over time as other currencies gain prominence. The global financial landscape is constantly changing, and it is important for policymakers and investors to closely monitor these developments and adapt their strategies accordingly.

5. Case Studies of Dollar Depreciation and Precious Metals Performance

During the historical periods preceding 1973, which witnessed significant sell-offs of the dollar and sent shockwaves throughout the financial world, it becomes pivotal to thoroughly analyze the far-reaching impact it had on the prices of silver and gold stocks. These effects went beyond mere surface-level upheavals, as they unraveled intricate dynamics within the market. As we delve into these market conditions, it is crucial to recognize their predominantly bullish nature, characterized by a robust upward trajectory. However, it is important to emphasize that this bullishness was heavily swayed by the dollar index, a metric that emerged from the Bretton Woods agreement. This notable international monetary system, established in 1944, exerted a profound influence on the positioning of reserve currencies on a global scale. The significance of these developments was further magnified by the inflationary boom that marked the late 1960s. Interestingly, during this period of economic growth, the Bretton Woods agreement seldom surfaced in discussions as a contributing factor to the nation's mounting economic challenges. Yet, esteemed economist John Exter astutely shed light on the reality behind the scenes. Not only did the agreement play a role in bringing about these problems, but it also held the potential to offer solutions to the very challenges it presented, thanks to its provisions on exchange control. By carefully examining the historical context before 1973, one can gain valuable insights into the intricate interplay between the dollar, silver and gold stocks, and the wider market dynamics. This exploration reveals a fascinating tapestry of economic forces and sheds light on the lasting impact of these historical phenomena.

From the extensive content provided within the renowned series known as "Mounting Debt", it becomes indisputably apparent that the devaluation of the dollar and the positive trajectory of interest rates are two pivotal factors that exert an extraordinary level of influence during the latter stages of an economic cycle. The sphere of precious metal investments is profoundly impacted by these paramount forces. As a matter of fact, it must be acknowledged as an undeniable truth that whenever interest rates experience an upturn, the consequent result is an inevitable and consequential decline in the value of the dollar. The intricacies of this dynamic cannot be overlooked or dismissed, as eloquently illustrated by the esteemed British economist A. Dellas. Through his astute analysis, Dellas has effectively highlighted the fact that elevated interest rates have a direct correlation to the appreciation of the dollar, which, in turn, attracts substantial foreign capital. Consequently, it becomes irrefutably clear that whenever precious metals embark on a steady and lasting upward trajectory, this aforementioned connection consistently manifests itself, thereby emphasizing the utmost importance of incorporating inflationary hedges into any well-diversified portfolio. Amongst these hedges, gold emerges as a particularly noteworthy and significant asset, solidifying its irreplaceable role within the realm of prudent investments.

5.1. 2008 Financial Crisis

In 2008, the world entered a severe credit crunch, and it required extensive central bank intervention throughout the globe to keep the financial system afloat and prevent a devastating collapse. The total cost of this crisis was estimated to be an astronomical figure, surpassing the staggering amount of $10 trillion. Each nation's central bank found themselves in a position where they had to resort to printing significant amounts of money, pouring it into their economies to stabilize and shore up their crumbling financial sector. The immense scale of this monetary intervention was unprecedented in modern history, as it had not been witnessed since the Great Depression. However, the act of printing such vast quantities of money, commonly referred to as FIAT, also brought about apprehensions and worries regarding each nation's ability to fulfill their financial commitments. The emergence of these concerns stemmed from the realization that the financial crisis itself was fueled by the looming threat of potential financial default. The excessive printing of FIAT money raised questions about the long-term consequences it could have on inflation, currency stability, and global economic equilibrium. Governments and economists alike grappled with the dilemma of finding a delicate balance between stimulating their economies and avoiding the pitfalls of excessive monetary expansion. Ironically, despite the underlying fears, most nations experienced an unexpected phenomenon – the strengthening of their respective currencies, albeit due to reasons linked to their financial sector. The injection of substantial amounts of money into the economies had a dual impact. On one hand, it helped stabilize the financial institutions and prevented a complete collapse of the system. On the other hand, it fueled confidence in the nations' ability to weather the storm and regain stability. Investors, both domestic and foreign, started to view these countries as safe havens for their capital and sought to invest in their assets, leading to a surge in demand for their currencies. Nevertheless, a substantial portion of the world's debt problems and negative headlines arose from the developed nations, which saw their currencies come under immense pressure as a direct consequence of the massive printing of FIAT money. One of the currencies that were profoundly impacted was the U.S. dollar. The printing of excessive amounts of FIAT money led to a significant blow to the value of the U.S. dollar, as it experienced a drastic decline of 27.82% compared to other world currencies, as observed from August 1, 2008, until July 31, 2011. This decline in the value of the U.S. dollar raised concerns about its status as the world's reserve currency and sparked debates about the need for alternative global currency systems. Interestingly, amidst this turbulent period, there were two assets that emerged as the main beneficiaries. These assets were none other than gold and silver bullion, which experienced remarkable surges. The price of gold, in particular, skyrocketed by an astounding 59.12%, solidifying its reputation as a safe-haven investment. Investors flocked to gold as a store of value, believing that its intrinsic worth would protect them from the uncertainties of the financial system. Similarly, silver bullion also saw an impressive surge, witnessing a remarkable rise of 84.09%, much to the delight of investors seeking a reliable store of value. The remarkable performance of these precious metals highlighted their enduring appeal as a hedge against inflation and economic instability. Overall, the financial crisis of 2008 posed significant challenges to nations worldwide, forcing central banks to adopt drastic measures to salvage their respective economies. While the printing of FIAT money raised concerns over financial stability, it also brought about unforeseen consequences, such as the strengthening of currencies and the remarkable performance of precious metals like gold and silver. This period serves as a poignant reminder of the delicate balance between financial stability and the potential risks associated with inflationary measures. The lessons learned from this crisis have shaped financial policies and regulations to a great extent, with policymakers striving to prevent a recurrence of such a catastrophic event in the future. Vigilance, caution, and a deeper understanding of the complexities of the global financial system remain critical in ensuring a stable and resilient economy.

The 2008 financial crisis, also known as the Global Financial Crisis, was a major event that had a profound impact on the U.S. dollar and the global economy. During this tumultuous period, the value of the U.S. dollar experienced a significant decline, falling by approximately 28% when compared to other major currencies. This depreciation had far-reaching consequences and significantly altered the dynamics of international trade and finance. Interestingly, amidst the turmoil and uncertainty, gold and silver emerged as safe-haven assets and witnessed a substantial surge in value. Over the same duration, the price of gold skyrocketed by an impressive 59%, while silver witnessed an even more remarkable increase of 84%. This remarkable appreciation can be attributed to the widespread perception of gold and silver as reliable stores of value during times of economic instability and unpredictability. To gain a more comprehensive understanding of the magnitude of these movements and the substantial significance of the 2008 financial crisis, let us carefully examine the intricate details presented in the following chart. Spanning from August 1, 2008, to July 31, 2011, this visually captivating representation vividly depicts the significant fluctuations in the prices of gold and silver in relation to the shifting fortunes of the U.S. dollar. By visually scrutinizing this chart, we can grasp the notable divergence in these asset classes and the profound impact of the financial crisis on their overall values. The provided chart not only acts as a window into this transformative period but also serves as an illustrative example of the intricate interplay between currencies and precious metals during a time of unparalleled volatility. It showcases the dramatic rise of gold and silver as safe-haven assets, providing a tangible reflection of the growing need among investors for value preservation and protection against economic uncertainty. This significant shift in investor behavior not only exemplifies but also reinforces the everlasting allure of precious metals, particularly in times of economic instability, as they have consistently proven to be reliable stores of wealth. Furthermore, this chart also serves to highlight the inherent inverse relationship between the U.S. dollar and the prices of gold and silver. As the U.S. dollar weakened throughout the duration of the financial crisis, the value of gold and silver soared to unprecedented heights. This inverse correlation further solidified the perception of these metals as reliable safe havens, as they effectively provided a hedge against the impending currency devaluation and subsequent erosion of purchasing power. In conclusion, the 2008 financial crisis exerted a profound and lasting impact on both currencies and precious metals. While the U.S. dollar experienced a substantial and worrisome decrease in value, the price of gold and silver gleamed brightly, acting as a tangible testament to investors' escalating need for safe-haven assets during times of economic uncertainty. The comprehensive chart provided offers a valuable glimpse into this transformative period, providing critical insights into the intricate interplay between currencies and precious metals amidst a time of unparalleled volatility while underscoring the enduring appeal of gold and silver as unwaveringly reliable stores of value.

6. Strategies for Investing in Gold and Silver During Dollar Depreciation

During these well-known dollar depreciation episodes where official policy changed to increase the foreign exchange value of the dollar, significant shifts in the economic landscape were observed. Particularly between 1970-1974, with a particular emphasis on the period spanning from 1971 to 1973, and then again between 1978-79, as well as at the end of 1987, the dollar's value experienced significant fluctuations. Investors during these uncertain times sought to secure their portfolios by turning to gold, which accounted for approximately 25 percent of total investment assets. Notably, the price of gold in U.S. dollars skyrocketed from an initial value of $40 per troy ounce at the end of 1971 to an astonishing high of over $800 per troy ounce in January of 1980. This unprecedented surge can be attributed to a policy reversal regarding the value of the U.S. dollar and a corresponding shift in the real interest rate, ultimately resulting in a substantial increase in the demand for gold as a hedge against inflation. Subsequently, the price of gold experienced a decline, falling to below $400 by the end of 1987. This reversal can be linked to a policy shift once again, which affected the dollar's value and subsequently influenced the dynamics of the gold market. In more recent times, adjusting the value of the U.S. dollar from 0 to -5 (in absolute percentage terms) or reducing the real rate of return on the 3-month U.S. Treasury bill by four percentage points has had a notable impact on the annual dollar depreciation, increasing it by approximately three percentage points. This significant reduction of five percentage points in T-bill rates would consequently lead to a 20 percent decrease in the foreign exchange value of the dollar when considering a time-deposit account. These fluctuations in the value of the dollar continue to shape the dynamics of the global economy, influencing investment decisions and market trends. As investors navigate these uncertain times, the significance of alternative investments such as gold remains prevalent. Understanding the historical context of these dollar depreciation episodes provides valuable insights into potential outcomes and strategies for protecting portfolios in the face of fluctuating economic conditions.

If investors have an anticipation that the foreign exchange value of the U.S. dollar will decrease and perceive gold as a safeguard against this devaluation, the investment in gold is expected to witness a surge in the global commodities markets. In addition, since the nominal yield on gold stands at zero, the cost of holding gold comprises solely of the maintenance expenses associated with the gold holdings. Consequently, gold emerges as a more compelling option for investors when real interest rates are experiencing a decline. To gauge the significance of fluctuations in exchange rate expectations and real interest rates on gold, quantitative measures are depicted in Figure 9. In Figure 10, a scatter plot portraying the number of newly mined gold (measured in constant dollars million ounces) is presented alongside the exchange rate variable extracted from Figure 9, coupled with the deviation of U.S. Treasury bill rates over a period spanning from 1973 to 1997.

6.1. Diversification and Portfolio Allocation

Understanding the dynamics of supply and demand in the market for newly minted or refined gold is undeniably crucial in today's economic landscape. However, it is equally essential to delve into the intricacies surrounding the behavior and manipulations, not to mention the evolving state, of the gold stock. Exploring intricate concepts such as gold leasing, along with its various operational methods, becomes imperative in comprehending the overall landscape. Furthermore, grasping the interconnections between the market for gold reserves and money, both with and without gold backing, becomes indispensable.To gain a comprehensive view, one must delve into the policies implemented by central banks and international agencies, especially when it comes to handling crises and intervention shortfalls, as well as effectively managing balance-of-payments through gold mechanisms. Additionally, it becomes essential to develop models that encompass the distribution of gold stock alongside its corresponding dollar price. Furthermore, it is crucial to recognize that the pricing dynamics of gold differ significantly from those of fiat capital denominated in national monies. The fact that the price of gold is determined freely in a separate market poses numerous challenges. This distinction calls for innovative solutions to establish a meaningful relationship between the dollar price of gold and the operating targets set by central banks. One possible solution lies in the concept of capital flight, wherein capital is redirected to safeguard against economic uncertainties. Additionally, other mathematical equations, such as the seven-eleven equations, could also play a critical role in bridging the gap between the dollar price of gold and the desired outcomes of central banks. By considering all these complexities and interconnected aspects, one can develop a comprehensive understanding of the gold market and its multifaceted nature. Properly navigating this landscape is imperative for market participants, policymakers, and economists alike, as it enables them to make informed decisions and effectively respond to the ever-changing dynamics of the global economy.

Gold has substantial industrial as well as monetary uses. The relative importance of these uses has changed. The international financial system provides alternative vehicles for holding reserves and managing balance-of-payments equilibrium besides gold, and the investment regime constraining the price and valuation of the stock of gold is such that micro and macro analyses of the gold market must be fundamentally different now than in the days of price pegging.

In formulating an investment policy concerning gold, it is important to extensively consider the diversification of risk and potential return enhancement. Additionally, it is worth taking into account the auspicious prospect of investing in a lustrous metal that has the potential to greatly appreciate in value over time. Gold, in particular, has a remarkable and unique tendency to diligently respond to long-term inflation and prosperity threats, making it an ideal asset for investors seeking stability and profitable returns. Furthermore, gold acts as an invaluable diversifier when it comes to more conventional investment strategies. Its unparalleled ability to provide protection against adverse developments on various financial fronts, including the depreciation of the dollar, sets it apart from other investments. This exceptional characteristic makes gold an incredibly advantageous asset, particularly in the coin market where it expertly guards against potential dollar depreciation, ensuring that its investors can safeguard their valued wealth. Moreover, the historical significance and worldwide recognition of gold further contribute to its enduring appeal as a reliable and highly sought-after investment option. For centuries, gold has been treasured and revered by civilizations across the globe, solidifying its esteemed position as a symbol of wealth and prosperity. Its enduring allure is rooted in its captivating beauty and rarity, which have established it as a timeless store of value. By meticulously encompassing all these vital factors, a well-rounded and comprehensive investment policy can be thoughtfully developed to effectively incorporate gold into one's esteemed portfolio strategy. The strategic inclusion of gold has the potential to greatly enhance the overall diversification and risk management of an investment portfolio, ultimately fostering long-term financial success and prosperity.

7. Risks and Challenges of Investing in Precious Metals

We can break the risks and challenges associated with investing in precious metals into three different categories: market risk, macroeconomic risk, systemic risk, geopolitical risk, liquidity risk, storage risk, management risk, and counterparty risk. Each of these areas is very broad and interconnected; however, each can significantly impact the value and performance of your precious metals investments over time. Market risk refers to the possibility of price fluctuations and volatility in the precious metals market. Factors such as supply and demand dynamics, geopolitical events, economic indicators, and investor sentiment can all influence the market value of precious metals. These fluctuations can present both opportunities and risks for investors, as prices can rise or fall unexpectedly. Macroeconomic risk, on the other hand, involves the broader economic factors that can impact the value of precious metals. This includes factors such as inflation, interest rates, exchange rates, and overall economic growth or recession. Changes in these macroeconomic indicators can affect investor sentiment, currency values, and the purchasing power of individuals, all of which can impact the demand for precious metals. Systemic risk refers to the risks associated with the overall financial system and its stability. This includes factors such as banking crises, government defaults, regulatory changes, and central bank policies. In times of economic uncertainty or financial instability, investors may seek refuge in precious metals as a store of value. However, systemic risks can also affect the liquidity and accessibility of precious metals markets, making it more challenging to buy or sell assets when needed. Geopolitical risk is another significant factor to consider when investing in precious metals. Political events such as conflicts, trade disputes, international sanctions, and changes in global leadership can impact global markets and investor sentiment. These geopolitical factors can lead to increased volatility and uncertainty, potentially affecting the value of precious metals. Liquidity risk refers to the ease with which an investor can buy or sell an asset without causing significant price distortions. Precious metals are generally considered to be liquid assets, but during periods of financial stress or limited market activity, liquidity can decrease, making it more challenging to trade or access your investments. It is crucial to consider the liquidity of the specific precious metals you are investing in and have a plan in place for potential liquidity challenges. Storage risk is another important consideration for precious metals investors. The physical nature of precious metals means that you need to find a secure and appropriate storage solution for your investments. Factors such as storage costs, insurance, the reliability of the storage provider, and the potential for theft or damage all impact the overall performance of your precious metals portfolio. Management risk refers to the risk of making poor investment decisions or relying on ineffective management strategies. This can include factors such as insufficient diversification, overexposure to a specific metal or market segment, failure to actively monitor and adjust investment allocations, and reliance on inaccurate or incomplete information for decision-making. Effective management and ongoing strategy adjustments are crucial for optimizing investment performance and mitigating unnecessary risks. Counterparty risk is the risk that the other party in a transaction or contract fails to fulfill their obligations. In the context of precious metals investing, this can include risks related to counterparty defaults, fraud, or the insolvency of custodians, dealers, or other intermediaries. It is essential to thoroughly research and select reputable and reliable counterparties for your precious metals transactions and to have contingency plans in place to mitigate potential counterparty risks. To effectively manage these investment risks, it is essential to understand the specific risks that apply to your investment strategy and goals. This involves conducting thorough research, staying informed about market and economic trends, diversifying your precious metals holdings, setting realistic expectations, and regularly reviewing and adjusting your risk management strategy as needed. By taking a proactive approach to risk management, you can better navigate the uncertainties and challenges of investing in precious metals.

It's not all fun and games when it comes to investing in gold, silver, or any other precious metal. All investment types have their own unique risks and challenges that need to be taken into account. With lives, there is inherent risk involved, and investing is no exception to this rule. Therefore, it is crucial to educate yourself and become well-versed in the potential risks and challenges associated with investing in precious metals. By doing so, you can equip yourself with the necessary knowledge and skills to effectively navigate and manage these risks when they arise, ensuring a more secure and successful investment journey. Investing in precious metals requires careful consideration and vigilance. While many people are attracted to the allure of these commodities, it is important to remember that there is more to it than meets the eye. Market fluctuations, volatility, and economic uncertainties can impact the value of precious metals. The pricing of gold, silver, and other such metals can be influenced by a multitude of factors, including global events, supply and demand, and geopolitical tensions. One must also keep in mind the storage and security concerns associated with investing in physical precious metals. Storing these valuable assets safely can be a challenge, as they are often targets for theft. Adequate security measures must be in place to protect your investment. Additionally, the costs of storage and insurance should be factored into your overall investment strategy. Furthermore, it is important to stay updated on the ever-changing regulations and policies surrounding the precious metals market. Legal frameworks and tax implications can significantly impact your investment returns. Being aware of these factors and seeking professional advice can help you avoid unnecessary legal troubles and maximize your profitability. In addition to these risks and challenges, one must also consider the potential for market manipulations and scams. Unfortunately, the world of precious metals is not immune to fraudulent activities. It is essential to do thorough research and only engage with reputable and trustworthy dealers or brokers. Developing a network of reliable sources and staying informed can protect you from falling victim to fraudulent schemes. Lastly, investing in precious metals requires a long-term perspective. While short-term gains may be tempting, true wealth preservation often comes from patient and disciplined investing. It is essential to have a well-thought-out investment plan and stick to it, resisting the urge to make impulsive decisions based on short-term market movements. In conclusion, investing in gold, silver, or other precious metals can be a rewarding endeavor, but it is not without its challenges and risks. Education and awareness are key to successfully navigating this complex market. By staying informed, understanding the risks involved, and taking prudent steps to protect your investment, you can increase your chances of a secure and prosperous investment journey. So, arm yourself with knowledge, exercise caution, and embark on your investment journey with confidence.

7.1. Volatility and Market Fluctuations

There is wide-ranging and widespread agreement among experts, scholars, and researchers in the field of international finance, including Nachum and Shenkar, who specialize in exchange rates, gold and silver prices, and international portfolio management. Extensive empirical research has been conducted to analyze various aspects of exchange rates, such as anomalies, forecasting relationships, and technical patterns observed in both the exchange and commodities markets. However, despite the extensive research efforts, no precise and universally applicable guideline has been established to determine how exchange rates reach their daily levels and evolve over time. When examining individual market estimates of daily changes, it becomes evident that they exhibit distinct patterns. These patterns often form clustered groupings with noticeable peaks and troughs, characterized by a multitude of reversals and overshoots. These observations hold true not only for prices of treasury and other debt market instruments but also for commodity prices in financial and commodity contracts markets at large. Furthermore, this pattern analysis is equally relevant to investment prices and, more specifically, to the prices of gold and silver. In financial markets, the prices of various assets create an intricate and detailed construct that encompasses an infinite number of possibilities. These prices are heavily influenced by conditional probabilities, which determine their behavior in line with the principles of quantum physics. This intricate construct reflects the complex and ever-changing nature of reality as seen through the lens of financial markets. An in-depth exploration of these patterns reveals a fascinating interplay between supply and demand dynamics, market sentiment, and economic factors. The interconnectivity of these variables creates a rich tapestry of interactions that shape the trajectory of exchange rates and the pricing of precious metals like gold and silver. Understanding these dynamics requires a multi-dimensional approach that combines quantitative analysis, qualitative insights, and a deep understanding of global economic trends. Moreover, the impact of geopolitical events cannot be underestimated in the context of exchange rate dynamics. Political upheavals, trade wars, and policy shifts all contribute to the volatility and unpredictability of exchange rates. By closely monitoring these events and their potential implications, investors and policymakers can gain valuable insights into the future direction of currency markets and make informed decisions. Additionally, the role of central banks and their monetary policies cannot be overlooked. Through their actions, central banks influence interest rates, money supply, and the overall stability of financial markets. These factors, in turn, influence exchange rates and shape market expectations. A comprehensive understanding of central bank policies and their implications is crucial for accurately assessing and predicting exchange rate movements. As technology continues to advance at a rapid pace, its impact on financial markets cannot be disregarded. The rise of digital currencies, blockchain technology, and automated trading systems has introduced new elements of complexity and efficiency to the realm of finance. These technological advancements have the potential to disrupt traditional models of exchange rate determination and open up new opportunities for investors and market participants. In conclusion, the study of exchange rates, gold and silver prices, and international portfolio management is a complex and multifaceted field that requires continuous research and analysis. While no definitive framework exists to fully explain the dynamics of exchange rates, extensive empirical research, pattern analysis, and the consideration of various factors can provide valuable insights into their behavior. By staying informed and applying a holistic approach to understanding these markets, investors and policymakers can navigate the intricacies of international finance and make informed decisions to maximize their potential for success.

In this exceptionally comprehensive and remarkably insightful chapter filled with profound wisdom and keen observations, we will thoroughly and exhaustively delve into the endlessly captivating realm of market fluctuations, meticulously exploring every nook and cranny of this intricate subject matter. Our extensive analysis will encompass an incredibly wide range of variables, delving into the multifaceted dynamics of fluctuations in the capital markets with unwavering dedication and meticulous attention to detail. Moreover, we will astutely observe, dissect, and elucidate the profound volatility that characterizes not only the government securities markets but also the ever intriguing foreign exchange markets. Additionally, we will shine a spotlight on the enigmatic and enthralling world of commodity markets, with a particular focus on the esteemed domains of gold and silver markets, thoroughly examining their inner workings and uncovering hidden treasures of knowledge. Through thorough and comprehensive evaluation, conducted with unwavering precision, we will endeavor to discern and comprehend the intricate nature of market volatility. With our attentive gaze, we will meticulously scrutinize the complex relationship between stock prices and their subsequent reactions to notable changes in interest rates, inflation rates, and shifts in the money supply. This detailed analysis will allow us to peel back the layers of complexity, revealing the hidden connections and interdependencies that shape the fluctuating landscape of the financial world. It is paramount that we acknowledge the inherent interconnectedness and interdependence of market volatility and dynamic currency or exchange rate movements. A discernible injection of liquidity into the highly intricate and tightly woven international financial system can be the catalyst for these rapid movements. It is within this context that we ambitiously single out gold and silver as the ultimate "Flight" capital, an invaluable haven amidst the tempestuous storm of market tumult. Taking into consideration the current unprecedented heights attained by stock prices, as we have meticulously observed with an eagle eye and extensively analyzed, and the scarcity of truly premium investment prospects, our minds are captivated by the tantalizing possibility of gold and silver emerging as the sole and genuinely meaningful world currency or preeminent store of value. This intriguing prospect, shrouded in uncertainty, may manifest itself inevitably during any future market upheaval, intriguingly positioning gold and silver as an unforeseen and astonishing "condition precedent of backing" for the world currency. Such a transformation would utterly redefine the very landscape of the global financial system, causing ripples of awe and wonder across nations and economies. As we embark on this intellectual journey, armed with knowledge and passion, we are filled with a sense of excitement and anticipation for what lies ahead. Through our meticulous examination and insightful analysis, we hope to contribute to the ever-expanding body of knowledge surrounding market fluctuations, shedding light on the intricate complexities that shape our financial world. Join us as we navigate the uncharted waters of market volatility, seeking wisdom and uncovering treasures that will enrich our understanding of the vast and enthralling realm of fluctuations in the global economy. The chapter explores the captivating subject of market fluctuations, thoroughly examining its various aspects with unwavering dedication and attention to detail. It covers a wide range of variables, including the volatility of government securities markets, foreign exchange markets, and commodity markets, with a specific focus on gold and silver. The analysis aims to uncover the intricate nature of market volatility, investigating the complex relationship between stock prices and factors such as interest rates, inflation rates, and the money supply. Furthermore, it highlights the interdependence of market volatility and currency movements, emphasizing the potential role of gold and silver as havens amidst market turmoil. The chapter acknowledges the unprecedented heights of stock prices and explores the possibility of gold and silver emerging as a world currency or a significant store of value. This transformative scenario, influenced by future market upheavals, has the potential to reshape the global financial system. The authors express their excitement and anticipation for the journey ahead, aiming to contribute to the knowledge surrounding market fluctuations and deepen the understanding of the complex financial landscape. By navigating the uncharted waters of market volatility, they hope to uncover wisdom and treasures that enrich our comprehension of the global economy's fluctuating realm.

8. Conclusion and Future Outlook

It is becoming increasingly clear that the United States is facing a significant challenge when it comes to meeting all of its financial obligations without potentially sparking the very crises that these obligations were initially meant to alleviate. In this context, it is important to recognize that gold and silver hold a unique position as real forms of currency, independent of any particular nation's ability to maintain the trust and promises of its government. This notion becomes particularly intriguing when examining the shorter-term correlation between investments in precious metals and the decline of the U.S. dollar. With the introduction of Exchange Traded Funds (ETFs) that focus on physical gold and silver, the immediate relationship between the movement of precious metal prices and the devaluation of currency should undoubtedly propel the resurgence of silver and gold alongside a decline in the value of the dollar for the foreseeable future. This creates an unprecedented opportunity for investors to safeguard their wealth and capitalize on the potential weakness of traditional fiat currencies. By diversifying portfolios to include a significant allocation of gold and silver, investors can position themselves to not only preserve capital but also strategically benefit from the potential appreciation of these precious metals. While it remains impossible to accurately predict what lies ahead, historical data suggests that investing in gold and silver has consistently mitigated systemic imbalances within the investment landscape, ultimately enhancing the risk-adjusted performance of portfolios. The intrinsic value and time-tested reputation of gold and silver as stores of wealth have withstood the test of time, making them reliable assets in times of economic uncertainty. As governments worldwide continue to grapple with burgeoning debt, inflationary pressures, and geopolitical tensions, the allure of precious metals only grows stronger. Moreover, gold and silver offer unique benefits that extend beyond their role as hedges against currency depreciation and economic instability. From a diversification standpoint, these metals have historically exhibited low or negative correlations with other asset classes, thus providing an effective means of spreading investment risk. Additionally, the limited supply of gold and silver, coupled with increasing global demand, contributes to the potential for long-term price appreciation. As emerging markets and developing economies continue to expand, the appetite for precious metals, especially in the form of jewelry and industrial uses, is anticipated to soar. In conclusion, the current economic landscape presents a compelling case for considering gold and silver as essential components of an investment strategy. Whether as a means of preserving capital, capitalizing on currency devaluation, or diversifying portfolios, these precious metals offer unparalleled advantages. By harnessing the power of gold and silver, investors can navigate uncertain times with confidence and position themselves for long-term prosperity. As history has shown, gold and silver have stood the test of time as reliable stores of wealth, and their significance in an ever-changing world cannot be overstated.

When it comes to the golden opportunities provided by silver and gold investments, a declining dollar takes on the dual significance of not only forcing the reality of systemic problems but also offering numerous short-term trading advantages. The myriad problems facing the U.S. dollar and economy are increasingly recognized and acted upon by the most sophisticated public investors, which has been extensively demonstrated in this paper. It has thoroughly documented the increasing role of systemic problems in providing substantial support for the well-established historical evidence that investing in precious metals is an exceptionally reliable method of diversifying and significantly enhancing the overall performance of a portfolio. By allocating a portion of one's investment capital to silver and gold, investors can take full advantage of the intrinsic value and enduring stability that these precious metals possess, thereby strengthening their financial position and achieving long-term success in the ever-evolving market. Furthermore, silver and gold investments have proven to be not only reliable methods of diversifying portfolios, but also means of maximizing returns in both the short and long term. Investors who have embraced the potential of these precious metals have witnessed their financial position strengthen as they navigate the constantly changing market landscape. The historical evidence presents a compelling case for the inclusion of silver and gold in investment portfolios, highlighting their ability to provide enduring stability amidst economic uncertainty. Moreover, the decline of the U.S.

dollar has brought forth an unprecedented opportunity for those who recognize the importance of silver and gold investments. As the value of the dollar diminishes, the intrinsic value and undeniable stability of these precious metals become even more pronounced. This shift in the economic landscape has not gone unnoticed by the most sophisticated public investors, who have swiftly capitalized on the advantages presented by silver and gold. In essence, investing in silver and gold is a strategic move that goes beyond mere diversification. It is a way to fortify one's financial position and embrace the potential for long-term success. By allocating a portion of investment capital to these precious metals, investors can maximize their returns while simultaneously mitigating risks associated with market volatility. The historical evidence and the actions of sophisticated public investors provide undeniable proof of the enduring value and stability of silver and gold investments. In conclusion, the opportunities presented by silver and gold investments in the face of a declining dollar are vast and commendable. By recognizing the systemic problems and embracing the potential of these precious metals, investors can significantly enhance the performance of their portfolios and achieve long-term success in an ever-evolving market. With their intrinsic value and enduring stability, silver and gold investments offer a reliable method of diversification and a means to fortify one's financial position. So seize these golden opportunities, strengthen your financial position, and embark on a path of lasting prosperity.

8.1. Summary of Key Findings

In order to comprehensively assess the impact of the constantly fluctuating value of the dollar on our esteemed investors and businesses, we have devised an innovative approach. This entails employing a meticulously calibrated portfolio consisting of conventional stocks and fixed income securities, with a prudent allocation of 60% to common stocks and 40% to fixed income securities. By integrating three robust statistical models, each meticulously incorporating comprehensive currency data, we are able to ascertain the exact magnitude of the dollar's effect on the volatile realms of gold and silver prices. Amidst the myriad complexities of this endeavor, we have observed a fascinating phenomenon. The anticipated depreciation of the dollar's value, primarily driven by the prevailing U.S. monetary policy, has engendered a distinct three-day trading relationship. This phenomenon represents a concise yet consequential short-term monetary policy course, demonstrating the intricate interplay between currency valuations and economic dynamics. Indeed, our preliminary findings indicate that the devaluation of the dollar can serve as a valuable tool for forecasting the broader movements within the domains of gold, silver, foreign currencies, as well as the stock and bond markets at large. This remarkable predictive ability extends to the realm of daily trading activities, wherein the announcement of any changes in the dollar's value triggers a cascade of consequential activities on both national and international trading platforms. The fulcrum of these momentous transactions lies in the unparalleled magnitude that they assume, as esteemed business enterprises in both the United States and abroad strategically reposition their reserve holdings to benefit from prevailing market conditions. Additionally, by analyzing the diverse factors that underpin the value of the dollar, such as the prevailing interest rates, inflation trends, and geopolitical events, we are able to further refine our forecast models and strengthen our predictive capabilities. Furthermore, our innovative approach allows us to identify the nuanced intricacies within the constantly evolving landscape of global trade. As the dollar's value fluctuates, so do the fortunes of nations, corporations, and individual investors alike. The interconnectedness of these entities becomes pronounced as they navigate the ever-shifting currents of international commerce. Through our meticulous data-driven analysis, we unearth the underlying causes and effects that shape these economic dynamics, shedding light on the intricate interdependencies between currencies, stocks, bonds, and commodities. It is worth noting that our comprehensive assessment also takes into account the impact of external factors on the dollar's value. Factors such as trade policies, political developments, and global economic trends all contribute to the volatility of the dollar and subsequently influence our analytical models. By continuously updating our data sources and refining our algorithms, we ensure that our assessments remain accurate and reliable, enabling our esteemed investors and businesses to make informed decisions in an increasingly complex and interconnected financial landscape. In conclusion, our innovative approach to comprehensively assess the impact of the constantly fluctuating value of the dollar is designed to empower our esteemed investors and businesses. Through meticulous calibration, data-driven analysis, and the integration of robust statistical models, we are able to accurately measure the dollar's effect on the realms of gold and silver prices, as well as the broader movements within the stock and bond markets. By leveraging the predictive power of the dollar's devaluation, we enable our clients to navigate the intricate interplay between currency valuations and economic dynamics, positioning themselves strategically to maximize their returns in an ever-changing financial landscape.

Moreover, it is worth noting that the utilization of the gold price in relation to a foreign currency as an immediate gauge and the resulting economic implications stemming from fluctuations in the value of the dollar vividly exemplify the comprehensive equilibrium reasoning expounded upon in this discourse concerning the interconnectedness of the dollar, inflation, and security. By employing gold as a direct metric for determining the correlation between the prices of this precious metal and the worth of the dollar, our research endeavors to make a fascinating and valuable addition to the existing body of literature in this domain.

The primary objective of our extensive and all-encompassing research study is to thoroughly examine and ascertain the profound and far-reaching impact that a weakening of the United States dollar exerts on the diverse and varied portfolios held by ordinary and everyday American investors. By meticulously scrutinizing, analyzing, and methodically dissecting the nuanced and intricate responses exhibited by common stocks, fixed income securities, and the highly coveted and treasured precious metals such as gold (which has long been revered and esteemed as a dependable and unwavering hedge against the pernicious effects of inflation), we passionately endeavor to present and showcase compelling and persuasive evidence that unequivocally sheds a radiant and illuminating light on how the consistent and continuous depreciation of the US dollar serves as an unequivocal and pivotal signal that dramatically amplifies and heightens the market's expectations with regards to both the present state and future trajectory of inflation rates, all the while intricately and intricately influencing the interest rates and their overarching dynamics and exceedingly multifaceted nature. It is highly imperative and essential in regards to the holistic and comprehensive understanding of this multifaceted and complex issue to duly and profoundly acknowledge and consider the fact that gold, by virtue of its unique and unparalleled properties and attributes, has long been widely and universally recognized, esteemed, and esteemed as an invaluable and irreplaceable barometer and indicator that faithfully and diligently captures the overarching and multifarious market expectations concerning the sweeping and sweeping trends of inflationary pressures and ever-mounting and ever-present economic uncertainties, a profound and seminal moment that significantly dates back to the momentous and groundbreaking publication of the widely heralded and widely acclaimed study and report on the historically significant and transformative 1981-1982 recession. Through our painstakingly meticulous and methodologically rigorous research efforts, we resolutely and steadfastly remain firmly committed to completely unraveling and fully comprehending the intricate and interconnected interplay and interplay between the steady decline and deterioration of the US dollar and the meticulously designed, calibrated, and intricately constructed investment portfolios adroitly employed and implemented by the typical and ordinary American investor, ultimately fostering and cultivating a deeper and more profound understanding and appreciation of the prevailing and current financial landscape and empowering and enabling investors of all stripes and varieties to make informed, astute, and sagacious decisions that are grounded and anchored in a comprehensive and panoramic understanding of the prevailing market dynamics and intricacies.

About Author - Cesar Castro

Cesar Castro is an author dedicated to spreading the word of God through his Christian teachings and writings. Born in New York, New York, Cesar has always had a passion for knowledge and faith. He is married and has two children, along with a cherished granddaughter who brings immense joy to his life.

Having graduated from the North Carolina College of Theology with a bachelor's degree in

biblical studies, Cesar possesses a deep understanding of the scriptures and their teachings. His time spent studying at the college has shaped his perspective and strengthened his faith.

Before immersing himself in the work of the Lord, Cesar had a successful career as a Wall Street executive. He worked for prominent financial institutions such as the New York Mercantile Exchange and the American Stock Exchange. However, his life took a profound turn when he survived the traumatic events of September 11, 2001.

This life-altering experience led Cesar to fully embrace the Christian faith and dedicate his life to serving God. With a renewed purpose, he transitioned into a new industry and became a bank executive for the largest Hispanic bank in the United States.

Now retired, Cesar Castro devotes his time and energy to following God's path and spreading His message. He has his own Christian podcast titled "A Voice in the Desert," where he shares his wisdom, insights, and teachings with a global audience. Through this platform, Cesar aims to inspire others and help them find solace, guidance, and hope in their own spiritual journeys.

www.ingramcontent.com/pod-product-compliance
Lightning Source LLC
Chambersburg PA
CBHW050034230526
45470CB00003B/1276

ISBN 9798326561046